Nature Did It First

Engineering Through Biomimicry

By Karen Ansberry • Illustrated by Jennifer DiRubbio

Dawn Publications

Burr

Have you ever walked your dog across
A field or weedy yard?
Maybe a Poodle, Labradoodle,
Boxer, Beagle, St. Bernard?

But when you got back home you found
That burrs were everywhere!
Stuck on your dog, hooked on your socks,
And tangled in your hair!

Nature Did It First—Hooks that Cling

Hitchhikers

Why do some plants have burrs? Burrs contain the plant's seeds. When a person or animal brushes against a burr, it comes off the plant and sticks to clothing or fur. The burr is then carried around until it falls off. The seeds inside fall out and grow new plants. So, when you have a burr on your sock, you are helping a plant spread its seeds!

A Closer Look

Why do burrs stick so well? If you touched one, how would it feel? Take a closer look with a hand lens. You will see a tiny, curved hook at the end of each spine. These little hooks help the burr latch onto fur, feathers, or fabric.

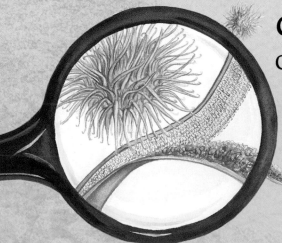

Copycat

George de Mestral lived in Switzerland. He liked to walk in the mountains with his dog. One day he noticed burrs sticking to his dog's fur. George wondered, "What makes them stick?"

When he looked at a burr under a microscope, he discovered their tiny, curved hooks! George was an **engineer**. He began thinking about how he could mimic, or copy, the way a burr works. What everyday problem could it solve?

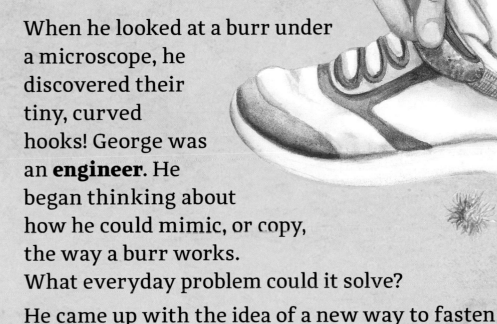

He came up with the idea of a new way to fasten things. His invention had tiny hooks combined with loops of fabric. In 1955, George named this new hook and loop **technology** "Velcro!"

Biomimicry

Velcro is an example of **biomimicry**—copying nature to help solve a human problem. Biomimicry helps people invent new things that improve our lives without harming Earth.

What other problems could be solved by mimicking burrs?

Little Brown Bat

Brown Bat wakes to hunt for prey
When daytime turns to night.
She has a trick to find her food
Without the use of sight.

She calls with little clicks and chirps
And hears if they bounce back.
The echoes help her catch a moth—
A tasty midnight snack!

Nature Did It First—Echolocation

Fly by Night

Little brown bats are small—only about 4 inches long. They have tiny, dark faces and rounded ears. Their fur is glossy brown. Like almost all bats, they are nocturnal. They hunt for food at night. Did you know that bats are the only mammals that can fly?

Insect Eaters

You might see little brown bats fluttering through the air at dusk or dawn. They are searching for moths, mosquitoes, and other insects. Bats help farmers because they eat pests that damage crops. One little brown bat can eat thousands of insects a night!

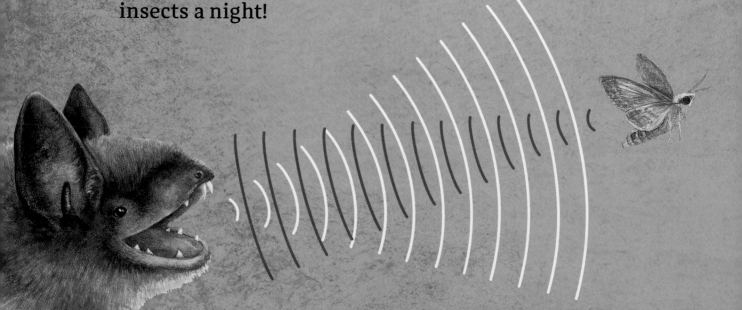

Echo! Echo!

Maybe you have heard the saying, "blind as a bat." But bats are not blind at all! At night, however, their ears are more important than their eyes. A little brown bat sends out high-pitched sounds as it flies. When the sounds hit an object (like a moth), they bounce back. The bat can tell where things are by listening to these echoes. **Echolocation** helps bats find their food. It also keeps them from running into things in the dark!

Making Life Better

Studying how bats find their way in the dark gave engineers an idea. They wanted to help people who are blind, so they designed a special cane. The cane mimics how a bat uses echolocation. It sends out high-pitched sounds. The sounds bounce back when they hit objects. Then the handle of the cane shakes. The user feels these **vibrations** and can tell when things are nearby.

What other problems could be solved by mimicking bats?

Gecko

If you've ever seen how geckos
Climb a tree or scale a wall,
You may have wondered why they
Never slip or slide or fall.

Well, geckos have a secret
That helps them stick like glue—
Their toes have tiny, clinging hairs!
Is that why they don't wear shoes?

Nature Did It First—Stick and Un-stick

Leaping Lizards

Geckos are a type of lizard. They have bumpy skin, which comes in many beautiful colors and patterns. There are over a thousand different kinds of geckos around the world. All geckos are good at running and jumping. Many kinds of geckos have another amazing superpower—climbing!

Hunting High and Low

Geckos that are good climbers can search for prey in all kinds of places. They can go up tree trunks looking for beetles. They can scurry along branches hunting bugs. They can crawl up walls in search of spiders. Some can even crawl upside down on ceilings! "House geckos" are welcome visitors because they catch pests like moths and mosquitoes. Would you want a gecko living in *your* house?

Mission Impossible

Geckos have a secret—their toe pads are covered in grooves. These grooves are lined

with thousands of tiny "hairs." Each hair branches out into more, even smaller hairs. The microscopic hairs allow a gecko to stick tight to surfaces. And when the gecko wants to move, it simply "unpeels" its toes and takes a step.

Sticky Solutions

It took scientists a long time to understand how geckos can stick and unstick to surfaces so easily. But once they figured it out, they worked with engineers to mimic the way a gecko uses its hairy toes. They invented a new kind of **adhesive**.

This super-adhesive is used in products like Geckskin®. A wall hook made of Geckskin sticks firmly to almost any surface and is strong enough to hold your backpack. When you want to remove the hook, it peels off easily without damaging the wall.

What other problems could be solved by mimicking geckos?

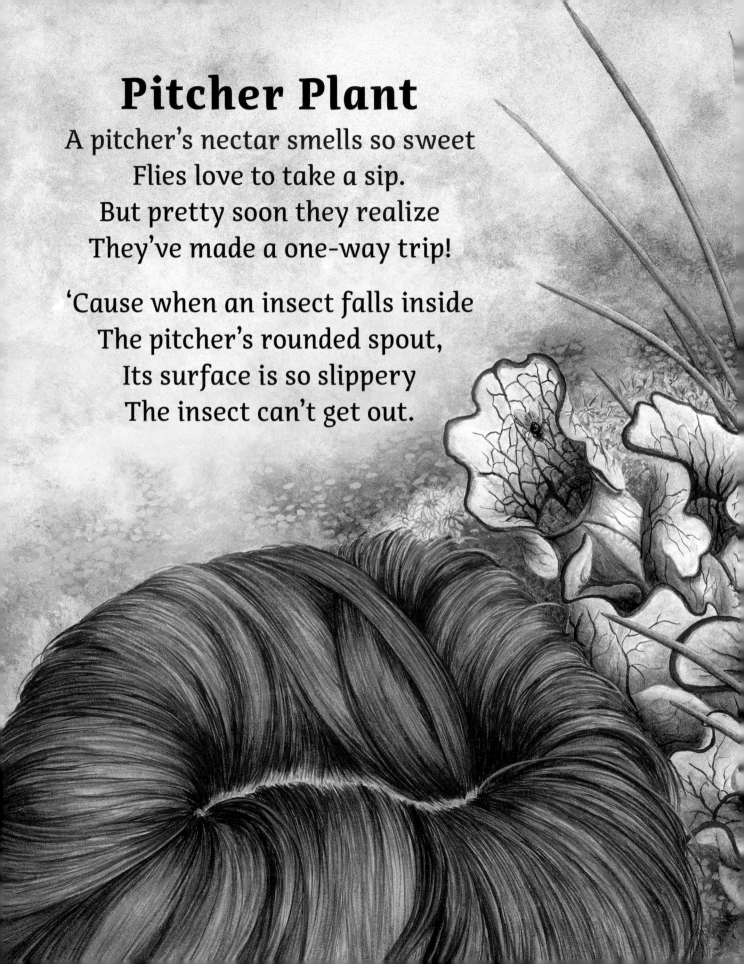

Pitcher Plant

A pitcher's nectar smells so sweet
Flies love to take a sip.
But pretty soon they realize
They've made a one-way trip!

'Cause when an insect falls inside
The pitcher's rounded spout,
Its surface is so slippery
The insect can't get out.

Nature Did It First—
Super Slippery Surface

Meat Eater

Pitcher plants come in many different colors, shapes, and sizes. But they all have one thing in common—they are **carnivorous**! Why would a plant need to eat meat? Like all plants, a pitcher plant makes its own food using air, water, and sunlight. But these plants have a problem to solve. They grow in poor soil that doesn't have some minerals the plant needs. So, a pitcher plant gets minerals from the bodies of insects.

A Slippery Slope

A pitcher plant attracts insects with its bright colors and sweet-smelling nectar. Insects land or crawl inside the hanging pitcher (which is actually a special leaf). The inner surface of the leaf is *very* slippery, and insects slide down into a pool of liquid. They can't crawl back out to safety, and they drown. Chemicals in the liquid digest the body of the trapped insect. The minerals from the insect's body can then be used by the plant.

Problem Solver

It takes many parts of the pitcher plant working together for the plant to get the extra minerals it needs from insects—fragrant nectar, cup-shaped leaf, slippery surface, and pool of liquid. Problem solved!

A Slick Invention

A team of engineers also had a problem. They were trying to invent a new, super-slick surface. They looked to nature for ideas and found out about the pitcher plant's leaf. Mimicking the leaf's slippery surface helped them design a new material. It can be used for lots of practical things. Lining a bottle with it helps ketchup slide right out! Someday it might be used to coat airplane wings in winter so ice will slide right off!

What other problems could be solved by mimicking pitcher plants?

Humpback Whale

Humpback whales are known as
"Ballerinas of the Sea."
Although these whales are super-sized,
They've great agility.

Their bumpy flippers help them swim
In circles to trap prey.
They gulp up tons of fish and krill—
An "all-you-can-eat" buffet!

Nature Did It First—Flippers with Bumps

Ballerinas of the Sea

Why are humpback whales nicknamed "ballerinas"? These giant mammals are bigger than a school bus! Yet they are graceful swimmers. They leap out of the water and twirl in the air. Humpbacks are slow movers, but they can swim in very tight circles.

Big Eaters

Humpbacks eat small fish and krill. A group of humpbacks will sometimes work together to catch prey by creating a "bubble net." They use their flippers to turn in tight circles. As they rise, they blow bubbles that form a ring. Schools of fish or krill

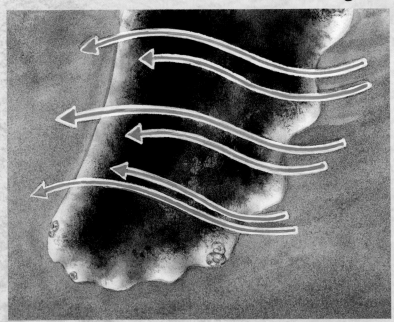

get caught inside the ring. The humpbacks can then gulp huge mouthfuls of food. One humpback whale can eat over a ton of food a day!

Bumpy Flippers

Humpbacks have the longest flippers of any whale. One edge of each flipper is covered in large bumps. You might think bumpy flippers would make the whale clumsy. But scientists have discovered something amazing! When sheets of water pass between the bumps, the whale's body can move more easily through the water. Despite their enormous size, they can make very tight turns.

Smooth Movers

Whale flippers reminded engineers of windmill blades. Whale flippers push against the water and windmill blades push against the air. Using biomimicry, engineers designed windmills with bumpy blades. The bumps help the blades turn more smoothly in the wind.

A surfboard company liked the idea of bumps, too. They invented a new kind of surfboard with a bumpy fin that turns better in the water.

What other problems could be solved by mimicking whales?

Pill Bug

Pill Bug is like a tiny knight
Dressed up in shiny armor.
Although he looks belligerent,
He's quite the little charmer.

When threatened, Pill Bug doesn't fight
Or try to run away.
He rolls up in a ball and waits...
Then goes about his day.

Nature Did It First—Rolling into a Ball

Crusty Crustaceans

Pill bugs are not bugs. In fact, they are not insects at all. Pill bugs are **crustaceans**, like lobsters, crabs, and shrimp. But pill bugs don't live in the ocean. They live on land. You can often find them under logs or rocks, where it is dark and damp. Although pill bugs might look ready for battle, they are harmless animals that eat mostly rotting plants.

Roly-Polies

A pill bug has a hard outer covering with seven overlapping plates. These plates are like armor. They can slide back and forth. When a pill bug is touched or feels threatened, it rolls up into a tight ball with all of its 14 legs tucked inside. This is why pill bugs are sometimes called roly-polies!

Playing Defense

Why do pill bugs roll up? A pill bug is a gentle creature that does not bite or sting. It is not very fast. So rolling into a ball and holding still is its best defense against predators. Rolling up allows the pill bug to protect its soft underside. When danger has passed, the pill bug unrolls and crawls away.

A "Pillbot"

Pill bugs gave **roboticists** an idea for a fire-fighting robot. The "pillbot" is about the size of a large dog. It can carry water tanks and fire extinguishers.

This robot moves on six legs, like an insect. But it can curl itself into a ball, like a pill bug. When rolled up, the robot's fireproof armor protects the equipment inside. Someday these robots might be used to fight forest fires.

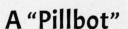

What other problems could be solved by mimicking pill bugs?

Kingfisher

The kingfisher sits upon a perch
And spies a silvery flash.
He swiftly dives to catch a fish
But barely makes a splash.

This bird's a diving champion
With gold-medal technique.
So what's the key to his success?
A super-streamlined beak.

Nature Did It First—Streamlined Shape

Champion Diver

The kingfisher is famous for its remarkable diving skills. It sits on a perch and watches for movement in the water. Once it spots a fish, it plunges headfirst into the water and quickly grabs the prey with its beak. Then it carries the fish back to the perch and swallows it whole!

Barely a Ripple

There are about 100 different kinds of kingfishers. Some live near water and eat mainly fish. Others eat things like insects, snails, and frogs. But they all have one thing in common—a long, sleek beak. Their beaks are so **streamlined** that a kingfisher can dive into the water and barely make a ripple.

BOOM!

The kingfisher's streamlined beak helped engineers solve a problem. In Japan, there is a type of super-fast train called a bullet train. The first bullet trains had rounded noses. When a bullet train entered a tunnel, the rounded nose would push the

air in the tunnel in such a way that it made a loud boom when the train sped out of the tunnel. It sounded like a thunderclap. People who lived near the train line complained about the noise. Something had to be done!

Serendipitous Solution

Luckily, the chief engineer was a bird watcher. He had seen how a kingfisher's unique beak could slice through the water without making a splash. He wondered if the same shape could help the bullet train slice through the air in a tunnel without making a loud noise.

The design team spent months creating a new nose for the train based on the shape of the kingfisher's beak. It worked—no more boom! By mimicking nature, the bullet train designers had solved their problem. Nature did it first!

What other problems could be solved by mimicking kingfishers?

Glossary

1. **Adhesive:** a substance used for sticking objects or materials together

2. **Biomimicry:** the process of designing nature-inspired solutions to problems

3. **Carnivorous:** (of animals) flesh-eating; (of plants) able to trap and digest insects and other small animals

4. **Crustacean:** a type of animal, typically living in water, with a segmented body, a hard outer shell, and several pairs of legs

5. **Echolocation:** the use of reflected sound waves (echoes) to locate objects

6. **Engineer:** a person trained and skilled in using science and math to design or invent things

7. **Roboticist:** a person who specializes in designing, building, and programming robots

8. **Streamlined:** having a shape that makes movement easier through air or water

9. **Technology:** a tool or machine designed to help solve a problem or meet a need

10. **Vibration:** a rapid back-and-forth movement

STEM Biomimicry Design Challenge

Bio means life. *Mimicry* means to imitate.
Biomimicry is the practice of imitating life to solve problems.

Give students an opportunity to become engineers with a STEM Biomimicry Challenge. They'll observe a plant or animal (photo, video, or in person) and describe its unique or interesting structures and functions. Based on what they observe, students can then identify a human problem that could be solved by mimicking the plant or animal, and then design an invention. Students will share the features of their invention by creating an advertisement for it.

 A "Teaching Guide" with complete step-by-step directions along with student handouts for grades K-2 and 3-5 are available as free downloads at www.dawnpub.com/activity/nature-did-it-first.

 Also available for students are printable handouts of the Glossary and a short bio of George de Mestral, the inventor of VELCRO®.

 For more valuable information and resources, go to the Biomimicry Institute (biomimicry.org) and Ask Nature (asknature.org). Discover nature's wisdom!

Karen Ansberry is a mom, teacher, writer, and nature lover. As the co-author of the *Picture-Perfect STEM* and *Picture-Perfect Science* series for elementary teachers, she gives workshops across the country helping teachers learn to integrate STEM and reading. Karen has taught science for over 25 years. Her science classroom was full of pets, including finches, rats, chinchillas, snakes, and even hissing cockroaches! Karen lives in historic Lebanon, Ohio, with her husband, four children, and three dogs. Find her at pictureperfectscience.com.

Jennifer DiRubbio has been drawing and painting throughout her entire life and has merged her passion for art with her passion for wildlife. Her mission is to help spread awareness and conservation for endangered wildlife. By creating works of art that capture the beauty of wildlife, Jennifer hopes to foster a love of nature in her audience. Jennifer is environmentally conscious in her art as well as in her home, where she lives with her husband and children. She donates a portion of her book royalties to support environmental organizations.

More Books by Karen Ansberry

 Teaching Science Through Trade Books, co-authored with Christine Anne Royce and Emily Morgan

Picture-Perfect series, co-authored with Emily Morgan:

 Picture-Perfect Science Lessons: Using Picture Books to Guide Inquiry, Grades 3-6

 More Picture-Perfect Science Lessons: Using Picture Books to Guide Inquiry, Grades K-4

 Even More Picture-Perfect Science Lessons: Using Picture Books to Guide Inquiry, Grades K-5

 Picture-Perfect STEM Lessons, K-2: Using Children's Books to Inspire STEM Learning

 Picture-Perfect STEM Lessons, 3-5: Using Children's Books to Inspire STEM Learning

Illustrated by Jennifer DiRubbio

 Going Home: The Mystery of Migration by Marianne Berkes

Mini-Habitat series by Anthony Fredericks:

 Under One Rock: Bugs, Slugs, and other Ughs

 In One Tidepool: Crabs, Snails, and Salty Tails

Near One Cattail: Turtles, Logs, and Leaping Frogs

On One Flower: Butterflies, Ticks, and a Few More Icks

Another Fun STEM Book from Dawn Publications

Scampers Thinks Like a Scientist—Scampers is no ordinary mouse! Her infectiously experimental spirit will have young readers eager to think like scientists too.

Dawn Publications is dedicated to inspiring in children a deeper understanding and appreciation for all life on Earth. You can browse through our titles, download resources for teachers, and order at www.dawnpub.com or call 800-545-7475.

Library of Congress Cataloging-in-Publication Data

Names: Ansberry, Karen Rohrich, 1966- author. | DiRubbio, Jennifer,
  illustrator.
Title: Nature did it first : engineering through biomimicry / written by
  Karen Ansberry ; illustrated by Jennifer DiRubbio.
Description: First edition. | Nevada City, CA : Dawn Publications, [2020] |
  Audience: Ages 5-11.
Identifiers: LCCN 2019013158| ISBN 9781584696575 (hardcover) | ISBN
  9781584696582 (pbk.)
Subjects: LCSH: Biomimicry--Juvenile literature. |
  Nature--Miscellanea--Juvenile literature. | Technological
  innovations--Juvenile literature. | Engineering design--Juvenile
  literature.
Classification: LCC TA164 .A5575 2020 | DDC 602--dc23 LC record available at https://lccn.loc.gov/2019013158

Acknowledgments

Special thanks to Emily Morgan for her encouragement and to Dr. Bill Robertson
for his careful attention to scientific details.

Special thanks to Erika Kuciw (aka Shuttergirl) for taking the reference photos of all my models.—JD

Book design, 3D illustrations for the nonfiction pages for each plant or animal,
and computer production by Patty Arnold, *Menagerie Design & Publishing*

Interior Fonts: Adagio Serif Script, Acme, and Adagio Serif
Cover Fonts: True Sketch and Chelteham Bold Condensed
Illustrations: Watercolor

Manufactured by Regent Publishing Services, Hong Kong
Printed January 2020 in ShenZhen, Guangdong, China

10 9 8 7 6 5 4 3 2 1
First Edition

Dawn Publications
12402 Bitney Springs Road
Nevada City, CA 95959
800-545-7475
www.dawnpub.com